Appliqué and Beyond

by

Annette Morgan & Bailey Curtis

ISBN 0-9541419-2-X
Published by Bailey Curtis

BAILEY CURTIS

7 LANCASTER TERRACE
NEWENT, GLOS. GL18 1EA

TEL. 01531 828664
www.baileycurtis.com

United Kingdom

Dedication

I would like to dedicate this book to the ones who have always encouraged me to fulfil my potential - my parents Heather and John Peaurt, my husband Dan and also Joel and Louise............and also to Jenny Daniels my City and Guilds Tutor who was a great inspiration and set me on this road of discovery and exploration!

Annette Morgan

Dedication

To the memory of my Aunt, Nancy, who fostered in me a love of textiles from an early age. Plus two other aunts, Evie and Con who also helped to teach me to sew, knit and crochet as a child. I am passing on these textile skills to my granddaughter who is a keen learner.

Bailey Curtis

Credits

Book design	word4word design & publishing ltd
Photography	Bailey Curtis
Other photography credits as stated	
Proofreading	Wendy Watts

Mission Statement
Our aim is to inspire your creativity and help you produce beautiful textile work.

Published by Bailey Curtis ISBN 0-9541419-2-X

Bailey Curtis
7 Lancaster Terrace
Newent, Glos GL18 1EA
Tel. 01531 828664
www.baileycurtis.com

Printed by PPL
Longcross Court
City Road (at Newport Road)
Cardiff
CF 24 3DJ

1 'Fiery Forest Autumn' by Bailey Curtis
2 'Rain Gods and Plume Serpents' by Alicia Merrett
3 'Boulder Sunrise' by Annette Morgan

1

4

2

3

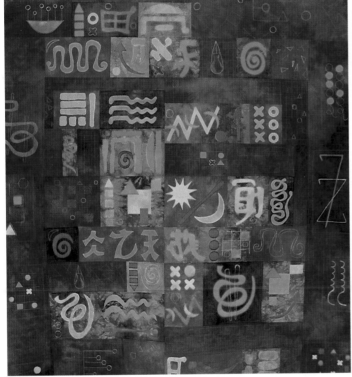

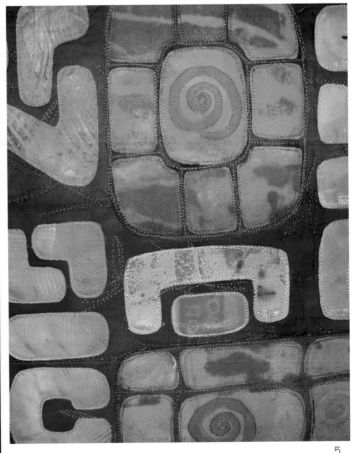

5

1 'Gatehouse' by Annette Morgan
2 'Elements of Magic' by Alicia Merrett
3 'Mining Memories' by Annette Morgan
4 'High Summer' by Eleanor Soar
5 'Stargazers of Uxmal' Detail by Alicia Merrett

1 'Romeo and Juliet' and photo by Linda Straw
2 'Mining Memories' by Annette Morgan

Introduction

I have always loved appliqué and developed my own ways of doing things before I knew how to do it "properly"! When the children were small I used to make all their clothes, and mine too, plus toy bags and birthday and Christmas gifts for friends. When I started City & Guilds Patchwork, Quilting and Appliqué I loved the appliqué sessions, especially the cutback and reverse appliqué techniques.

For several years now I've wanted to write a book, and have been encouraged by numerous students on the appliqué courses to do just this. I mentioned this to Bailey when she was writing her last book "Inspiration to Stitch" and we agreed to collaborate.

...So here it is, a book that covers a wide range of techniques with lots of tips and I hope lots of inspirational ideas and images for you to view.

My thanks to students past and present especially my City & Guilds students who never fail to inspire and excite me. Special thanks to Eleanor Soar, Allison Smith, Jennie Collins, Delia Cecil, Chris O'Dowd and Janet Valentine who lent their work for this book, and to my quilting penfriend Kathy Cruthirds who made my appliqué sewing machine cover, who despite my lack of communication still writes to me!

Annette Morgan

Appliqué is such a clever way of manipulating fabric. There are so many different ways of using it. We have gone through the stages and techniques in an easy to follow format helping you to use this book to further your knowledge of applying fabric. There are many examples of appliqué work from textile artists, embroiderers and quilters to also inspire you.

I have used appliqué in my own work for many years without giving a thought to the various other ways of applying one fabric to another. So this book is useful to me too, with Annette's helpful suggestions for using this technique.

Thanks to all of you who let me photograph your work; Delia Blackman, Sylvia Grant, Val Holmes, Linda Kemshall, Penny Maishman, Alicia Merrett, Madeleine Millington, Jan Mortimer, Janice Myers and Teresa Searle.

Lastly, a big thanks to Annette for making all the wonderful samples.

Bailey Curtis

1　'Forest Glade' by Annette Morgan
2　'Africa II' whole quilt by Annette Morgan

Simple Basic Appliqué

Simple basic appliqué is where fabric is applied directly to the background fabric. Raw edges can be a feature of this work and interest can be added by using brightly coloured machine embroidery threads. Make a mix of textures and colours by using scraps from your scrap/bits bag - use glitzy or shiny fabrics too, anything goes!

Method

◎ Select a background fabric - a firm close weave fabric is best to give stability.
◎ Cut out shapes which can be drawn out onto paper first.
◎ Lay your shapes, scraps or strips on the background fabric and pin in place - you can use a fabric glue or stick glue to hold the pieces in place if you prefer.
◎ Machine stitch about ¼ inch away from the edge of the fabric scraps and continue until all the edges are secure.
◎ Take machine threads through to the back of the fabric and secure.

Tips
• Fabric glue or stick glue can be used to anchor fabric pieces in place.
• If a background fabric puckers when appliquéing, place the fabric onto a piece of paper and stitch through all layers or try 'Stitch and Tear®' or 'Golden Threads Quilting Paper,®' these products can provide stability and stop the puckering effect.

Hand Method

This method of appliqué can be done by hand using a running, chain or blanket stitch, but secure fabric in a hoop to eliminate puckering.

Stitches

Straight stitch, zig-zag stitch, blanket stitch, chain stitch.

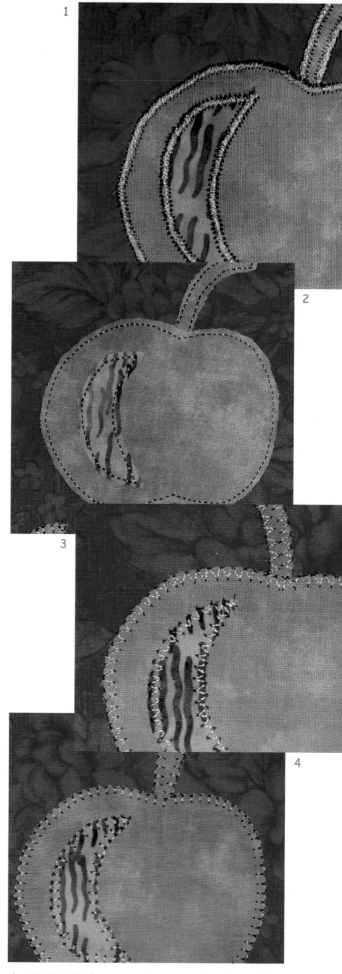

1 Satin Stitch
2 Straight Stitch
3 Zig zag Stitch
4 Blanket Stitch
5 Simple Appliqué on an Indian Jacket

Basic Appliqué Using Iron-On Vilene

This method is fairly simple providing you place the shiny side of the vilene onto the back of the fabric you want to apply - see tips below. The vilene gives stability to the appliqué shape and enables you to position the shape before pinning or using fabric glue. It also gives a softer feel than the bonding method (page 8) and provides an edge that frays less than with basic appliqué.

Method

◎ Select a background fabric as before.
◎ Iron the iron-on vilene onto the fabrics selected - shiny side of vilene to the wrong side of the fabric - see tip below.
◎ You can draw onto the see-through vilene, but draw on the matt side if you don't want the shape to come out back to front.
◎ Cut out desired shapes and place onto background, pin or glue in place.
◎ Stitch round each section with plain or decorative stitches.
◎ Take machine threads through to the back of fabric and secure.

Tips
• Use an old iron when using vilene and bonding agents.
• You can use baking parchment between iron and vilene which will prevent iron getting sticky.
• Iron vilene onto a larger piece of fabric to avoid problems of stickiness on your iron.
• Place vilene over a drawn shape first before ironing onto fabric then you have the piece ready to cut out - remembering that it will be in reverse!
• Use lightweight or medium weight vilene.

Hand Method

Once secured with pins or glue, place fabric in a hoop and use blanket stitch or other embroidery stitches to hold motifs in place.

Stitches

Straight stitch, zig-zag stitch, blanket stitch.

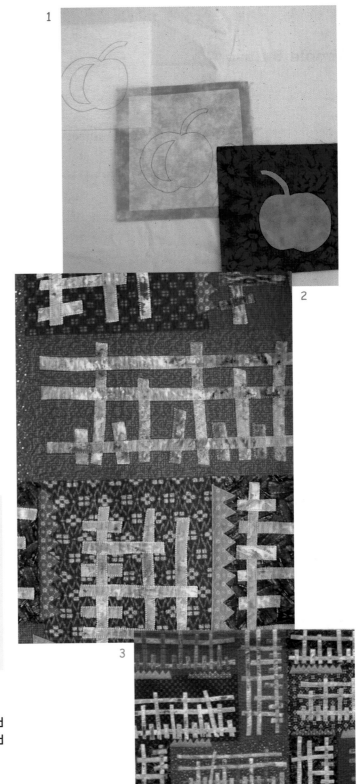

1 Iron-on vilene
2 'Charlcote Fences' Detail by Annette Morgan
3 'Charlcote Fences' by Annette Morgan
4 'Africa II' detail by Annette Morgan

7

Bonded Appliqué

There are various products on the market available for bonding one fabric to another they include 'Bond-a-Web'®, 'Heat-n-Bond'® and Pellon 'Wonder-Under'® to name a few. Some are lighter than others and give a softer handle to the fabric.

You may want to experiment to see which best suits your needs.

Bonding agents can stick to your iron and ironing surfaces, so keep an old iron specifically for this method and cover your ironing surface with an old piece of fabric!

The bonding agent is a web of glue which sits on a backing paper - try peeling a corner away. You will need to cut through the paper and the bonding agent in order to apply it to the fabric.

Method

◎ Select a background fabric as before.
◎ Iron a square of bonding product onto a larger piece of fabric to avoid problems of stickiness on your iron.
◎ Cut out your shape from the bonded fabric, peel off the paper backing and place on your background fabric and iron in place.
◎ Sew round each section with plain or decorative stitches.
◎ Take machine threads through to back of fabric and secure.

Tips
• Use an old iron!
• Peel the bonding agent away from the backing paper and use small pieces to bond shapes to a background, rather than use a whole sheet.
• Paint a sheet of 'bond-a-web' with acrylic paints and inks, when dry cut out shapes and apply to fabric with an iron, peel off backing and you are left with a textured surface.
• Use this method for Broderie Perse (see page 10).

Stitches

Straight stitch, zig-zag, blanket and satin stitch.

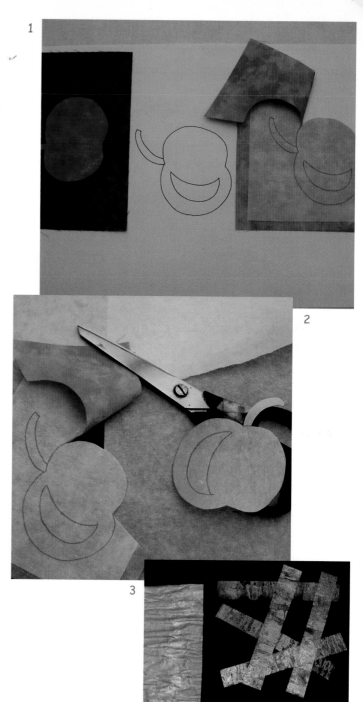

1

2

3

4

1   Bonding Product
2   Bonding Product
3   Painted 'bond-a-web'
4   Silver Birch by Annette Morgan

Bonding Powder

Bonding powder comes in tubs and is usually used for turning up hems and repairing garments. This is a similar product to bonding agents but in a powder form.

It is useful in appliqué techniques for bonding small pieces of fabric in place.

Method

◎ Choose a background fabric - avoid strong dark colours, as the powder will show up as tiny white dots.
◎ Sprinkle the bonding powder over the background fabric.
◎ Scatter tiny pieces of fabric and or threads (confetti) over the base fabric.
◎ Cover fabric with baking parchment and iron.
◎ Remove parchment and shake base fabric to remove excess confetti.
◎ Stitch using free machine embroidery/quilting and use a variety of machine threads.

Tips
• Most supermarkets have Teflon® sheets for lining cooking tins, these can be used in the same way as baking parch ment and last forever!
• Save threads and fabric to make the confetti.

Stitches

Use free machine embroidery, use a zig-zag or set machine embroidery stitches.

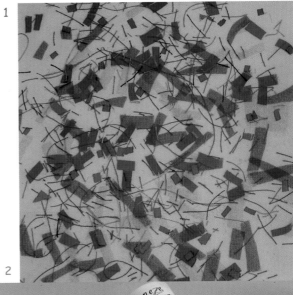

1 Confetti
2 Bonding Powder and Sample
3 Design Board by Eleanor Soar
4 High Summer by Eleanor Soar

Broderie Perse

Broderie perse is a technique that developed in the 16th and 17th centuries due to the importation of glazed cottons and Indian chintzes. The dyes in these fabrics were fast and the brightly coloured fabrics were treasured; import of these fabrics was banned in 1701 due to the economic threat they posed to Britain's textile industry.

As a consequence these fabrics became rare. Needlewomen would cut out motifs from the painted fabrics and re-arrange them into new compositions. The craft was so popular that by the 1800s manufacturers of cloth began printing fabric specifically for broderie perse.

Method 1 - bonded

- As for bonded appliqué.
- Make a flower wreath or bouquet of flowers.
- Machine stitch.

Method 2 - turned in and stitched edge

- Cut out motifs allowing ¼ - ½ inch seam allowance all the way round the shape and clip the curves if needed.
- Place on background using pins, fabric glue, glue stick or small piece of bonding agent.
- Turn under edge and stitch with a tiny blind stitch.
- Embroidery stitches can be used to link areas and decorate edges such as chain stitch and stem stitch.

Hand Stitching

- Bring the needle up through the fabric and catch the edge of the appliqué shape.
- Take the needle down beside the appliqué, travel underneath and bring the needle up and repeat as above.

Tips
- Use a slightly darker thread for the appliqué, a lighter thread is more obvious.
- Use a fine sharp needle (straw needles) and just catch the edge of the fabric.
- A closely woven fabric is easier to apply than an open weave fabric.

1 & 2 Broderie Perse samples by Annette Morgan
3   Broderie Perse sample by Janet Valentine

Reverse Appliqué

Cut Back

This is a method of reverse appliqué where the design is revealed as the top layers of fabric are cut through to reveal the layers of fabric below.

Method

◎ Decide on the motif you wish to use, chose at least 3-4 pieces of fabric, bold contrasting fabrics work best.

◎ Draw the design on the top layer of fabric with pencil or chalk.

◎ Layer the other fabrics underneath and pin or tack together.

◎ Machine over the drawn lines using a small zig-zag stitch.

◎ Using small sharp scissors start cutting the top layer of fabric away to reveal the layers underneath, other layers can be cut back as required.

Variation

◎ Use a straight stitch to sew over the design.
◎ Cut the fabric layers back.
◎ Sew over the straight line with a satin stitch.

> **Tips**
> • If you have a sewing machine with a side fitting bobbin, it may have an arm with a small hole in the end - if you are doing a satin stitch put the thread through this hole after you have threaded the bobbin, it tightens the stitch to give a neater finish.

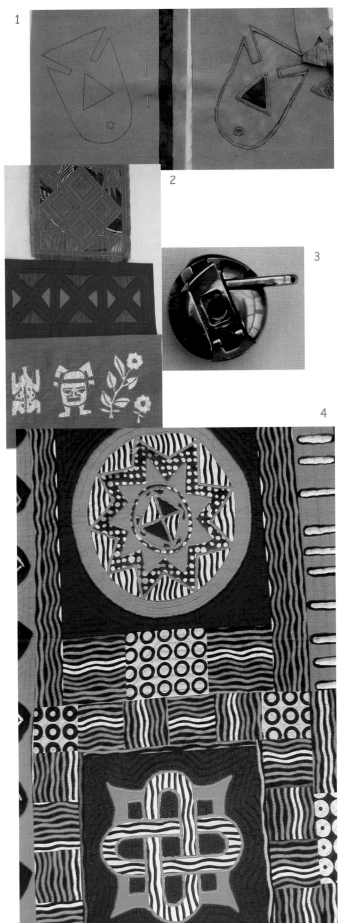

1 Reverse Appliqué method
2 Reverse Appliqué sample
3 'Bernina' Bobbin
4 'African Quilt III' Detail by Annette Morgan
5 'African Quilt III' by Annette Morgan

Hand Reverse Appliqué

This type of appliqué can be used to make Hawaiian appliqué, which is made from one piece of fabric. There is a theory that Hawaiian appliqué developed because the women on the islands saw the shadows from the palm trees on the ground and used these as designs in their work.

Method

◎ Make a snowflake paper pattern, fold a square in half, fold again diagonally from folded corner to the opposite corner and repeat second fold again.

◎ Cut into this folded section to create a snowflake design, making sure that the design has soft curved edges rather than pointed -this will make it easier to sew.

◎ Transfer this design to freezer paper and cut out design.

◎ Iron shiny side of freezer paper onto right side of fabric which is to be applied.

◎ Lay this fabric onto the background fabric and tack layers of fabric together, through the freezer paper.

◎ Starting at one corner of the design, cut through the top layer of appliqué fabric about ⅛ inch to ¼ inch away from the freezer paper, edge for about 2 inches.

◎ Using the paper edge as a guide & using a threaded needle, tuck the raw edge under the freezer paper and catch the edge of the appliqué fabric with a small stitch.

◎ Continue all the way round the shape just cutting a few inches ahead of where you are working, this prevents the piece of work from becoming misshapen.

◎ To sew the cut away areas in the centre of your design cut fabric away as required and proceed as above.

Tips
• Use a finely woven fabric for the appliqué, it will fray less and tuck under evenly.
• Use straw needles, which are very fine and use silk thread to produce an almost invisible stitch, this was recommended by Shirley Bloomfield (a stitcher from Suffolk, well known for her Baltimore appliqué).
• Use a thread slightly darker than your appliqué fabric - it will show up less.
• To make your stitches almost invisible bring the needle up through all layers just catching the edge of the appliqué fabric and bring the thread through, take the needle down at nearly the same point and move the needle underneath the backing fabric to the next point about ¼ inch away and repeat.

1

2

1   Hand Reverse Appliqué Sample
2   Containers made by City and Guild students from left to right Jug by Eleanor Soar, Tall Black Vase by Jennie Collins, Card Vase by Jennie Collins, Octagonal Bowl by Chris O'Dowd, Ivy Leaf Vase by Delia Cecil

Reverse Appliqué
Linda Straw's Method

Linda Straw is an embroiderer who is well known for her appliqué work and her special technique of reverse appliqué. She works from the back of the piece initially and then does exquisite embroidery on the front, using only silk fabric and a rayon thread to stitch her work. Linda often uses literary and historical subjects as inspiration.
  This is my interpretation of her technique!

Method

◎ Choose a motif and draw it out on paper.
◎ Lay a piece of non-iron-on vilene over the drawing and trace the design using a pencil or pen, this will be the back of the embroidery.
◎ Lay the vilene on some wadding, remembering to reverse the vilene if you have an asymmetrical design and then place the two layers on a piece of fabric, this will become the background fabric on the front of the quilted layer, pin the layers together around the edge.
◎ Place these layers on a piece of fabric chosen for the motif and pin or tack in place.
◎ Sew over the drawn line on the vilene using a free machine embroidery stitch.
◎ Turn over and trim the fabric away from the sewn line of the motif using a small sharp pair of scissors.
◎ This raw edge can then be covered with a satin stitch.
◎ Other fabrics can be applied in the same fashion to other areas of the design.
◎ Once this basic method has been learned you can design more complex patterns and use lots of different fabrics on the background.

1

1

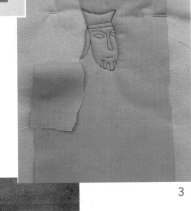

2

3

4

5

1 Image placed on wadding and backing fabric
2 & 3 Starting to stitch
3 Reverse of picture 2
4 'St Augustine' finished sample by Annette Morgan
5 'Romeo and Juliet' Detail and photo by Linda Straw

Freezer Paper Appliqué

Freezer paper has a silicone coating (the shiny side) which when ironed to fabric stays put, making it useful as an aid to appliqué. It can be removed easily and used again.

Method 1

◎ Cut out the shape to be used in freezer paper.
◎ Cut out fabric allowing ¼ inch fabric allowance all round the shape, and place the paper shiny side up on the wrong side of the fabric.
◎ Using one hand fold the edge of the fabric over onto the freezer paper and with the tip of an iron press the fabric onto the freezer paper.
◎ Stitch shape onto background fabric using a small invisible stitch.
◎ Cut a slit in the background fabric the back of the appliqué and remove the paper.

Method 2

◎ Cut out the shape to be used in freezer paper.
◎ Cut out fabric allowing ¼ inch fabric allowance all round the shape, this time the freezer paper will be on the right side of the fabric.
◎ Using needle turn stitching (turning the fabric under with the needle as you take tiny stitches) apply fabric to the background.
◎ Remove paper when the stitching is complete.

Tips
• Only cut small slits at the back of the appliqué to remove the paper, some people cut the background fabric behind the appliqué completely away which reduces the stability of the work.

Freezer paper has other uses

• Use as a stencil for fabric painting, cut a square of fabric and cut a shape out of the centre of freezer paper, iron to selected fabric and sponge fabric paint through the cut shape, remove paper when dry and iron to fix.
• Use as a stencil for screen printing.
• Use for foundation piecing, use an unthreaded sewing machine to punch the patterns, when sewing use the holes as a sewing guide.

1

2

3

1 Freezer paper 'Basket of Flowers'
2 Freezer paper appliqué sample
3 Freezer paper appliqué sample

Invisible Machine Appliqué

Use this method in conjunction with freezer paper. The appliqué stitches become invisible if you use a monofilament nylon (invisible thread).

Method

◎ Cut out a freezer paper shape (see method 1 in freezer paper appliqué), place the paper shiny side up on the wrong side of the fabric, allowing ¼ inch fabric allowance and iron the edge of the fabric down onto the freezer paper.

◎ Place onto background fabric, using a machine blind hemming stitch, stitch motif onto background fabric.

Tips

• Use invisible thread in the top of the machine and ordinary thread in the bobbin.
• Be careful ironing invisible thread, it can melt if the iron is too hot.
• Use a hemming foot to stitch, if you have one, on your machine.
• The width of the blind hemming stitch can be adjusted so the stitch just catches the edge of the appliqué fabric.

Inlay Work

Inlay work is a type of appliqué in which felt is used to give an inset effect. This method will give you a positive and negative design.

Method

◎ Select two pieces of contrasting fabrics, for example blue and yellow, and draw your design on both.

◎ Using sharp scissors cut out each motif, but keep the cutting line within the shape i.e. don't cut to the motif from the outer edge.

◎ Place the background of each piece of felt onto a cotton backing -this will make it easier to sew.

◎ Put the blue motif into the yellow felt and vice versa, each piece should fit snugly into the cut out shape, pin in place.

◎ Use embroidery threads to secure pieces together using a single running stitch or other embroidery stitches.

Variation

Use a large piece of felt and cut out areas of a design, place this onto a piece of silk, secure with a spray fabric adhesive and embroider with hand or machine stitches.

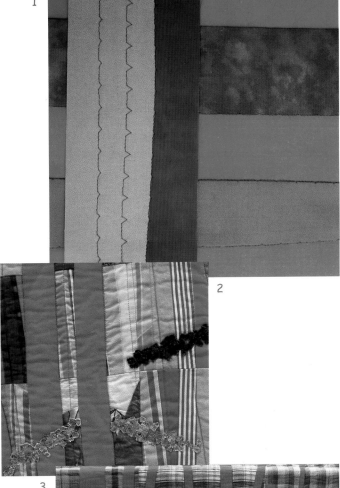

1 Invisible Appliqué
2 'Red Trees' Detail by Annette Morgan
3 'Red Trees' Whole Quilt by Annette Morgan
4 Inlay Sample by Annette Morgan

Bailey's Version of Appliqué

A much freer way of applying one fabric to another.

Method

◎ Paper pieces can be torn, or cut to represent the fabric to be applied.

◎ Pin these to the background where the fabric is to go.

◎ Cut out cotton scrim or other lightweight fabric for each piece of paper and replace the pieces bit by bit, pinning in place.

◎ The appliqué fabric is then stitched to a pre-made fabric background using a darning foot on your sewing machine and straight stitch with the feed dogs down.

◎ If you are sewing onto wool, choose a contrast fabric, such as cotton, viscose or linen for the appliqué. Always sew with pure cotton thread which also dyes. Once dyed with acid dye (for the wool) in one colour and direct dye (for the cotton) in a different colour, dyed in the same dye-bath, the fabrics contrast really well.

◎ After dyeing the scrim edges fray slightly giving a more fuzzy look.

◎ If you don't want to dye then use a contrasting light weight fabric against a heavier background fabric of a different colour. Wash the fabric well to get fuzzy edges if you want them.

Tips

• You can use a fabric pencil for drawing onto the appliqué pieces before sewing.

• For smaller pieces use the left over scraps.

• Viscose fabrics, velvet and satin work well with this technique.

• Once confident with this technique you can sew the cotton scrim straight onto the background fabric without patterns, cutting out the shapes after stitching.

• Lightweight silk works well, but will take the acid dye in the same colour as wool background.

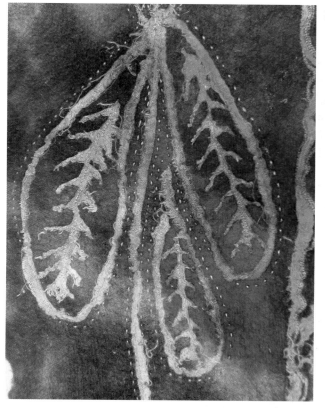

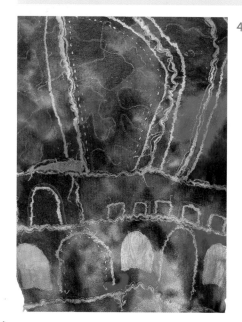

1 'Bodnant Garden' by Bailey Curtis
2 'Bodnant Garden' Detail by Bailey Curtis
3 'Powis Castle Gardens' by Bailey Curtis
4 'Powis Castle Gardens' Detail by Bailey Curtis

The method for making most of Bailey's quilt hangings is unusual as all the appliqué and stitching is done before dyeing. Using white hand-made felt, with cotton backing, fine cotton muslin or scrim is applied on top using a cotton machine thread. The piece is then dip dyed in two separate dyes, both in the same dye bath, one for the wool and another, in a different colour for the cotton.

The quilt "Over to You", was made by correspondence, - e-mails, samples and 'phone calls by two people who had never met.

Bailey mentioned to someone who was ordering dyes that there was a two-person quilt category at the first "Festival of Quilts" competition in 2003. Delia Blackman gamely volunteered to make a quilt with Bailey.

After the initial idea of using the botanical gardens as a theme, Bailey visited the one in Birmingham and Delia the one in Cambridge for inspiration. Samples were sent back and forth and eventually a design of Bailey's was agreed on and the stitching began. Delia made two lovely 'bark bits', which were all white and cream wool felt, silk and cotton. Bailey dip-dyed them both separately in shades of bright pink. Then the other sections arrived, made by Delia, out of white felt, stitched with cotton and viscose satin. Bailey stitched three pieces together to form a strip, three strips in all were dip-dyed in green shades for the wool parts with orange, pink and red for cotton and viscose.

The whole piece was then stitched together to form the finished quilt. Only after this did Bailey and Delia finally meet.

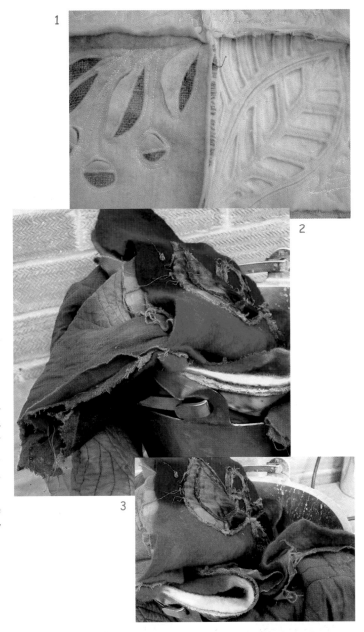

1

2

3

7

8

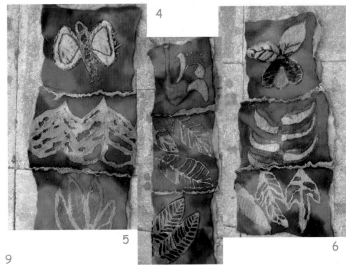

4

5

6

9

1   Undyed Sample by Bailey Curtis
2 & 3 Dyeing in Progress by Bailey Curtis
4, 5 & 6 Separate strips by Bailey Curtis and Delia Blackman
7 & 8 'Bark Bits' by Delia Blackman, dyed by Bailey Curtis
9   'Over to You' quilt by Bailey Curtis and Delia Blackman

Stained Glass Window Appliqué

As the name suggests this type of appliqué is based on stained glass windows and uses bias binding to cover the raw edges of the appliquéd fabric. Bought bias binding is usually very poor quality. Make your own with a bias making tool. Bias means cut diagonally across a square of fabric and not on the straight grain, in order for it to give. The lead used in windows extends to the edge of the window so the bias binding used to imitate the lead should also extend to the edge of the piece of work.

Method

◎ Select a design and draw it on paper, use this design as a pattern, and cut out the relevant sections in fabric, and place on your background, secure with pins or fabric glue.

◎ Make the bias binding by cutting strips of fabric on the bias, using a rotary cutter, mat and ruler - you could use a ruler and chalk and scissors - to the required width of your bias maker, usually 1½ inches wide.

◎ Thread the fabric strip through the bias maker using a pin to ease it through the channel and holding the fabric strip and the bias maker with one hand, iron the strip as it comes out of the bias maker with the other hand.

◎ Lay the bias with the flat side of the fabric downwards and trim away one side of the raw edge of the bias bind ing close to the ironed fold, so that you have a thin raw edge and a wider raw edge (this takes away some of the bulk) and fold in half, the bias is now ready to apply.

◎ Apply the bias by covering the raw edge of the pattern pieces, remembering to cover the small areas first, as larger areas of the bias can cover the smaller areas.

◎ Sew using an invisible appliqué stitch by hand, or use a sewing machine with a small zig-zag or invisible hem stitch.

Tips
• Try other colours of bias binding, grey. red, navy blue or patterned fabric.

1

2

1 Stained Glass sample by Annette Morgan
2 'Stained Glass' by Anne Crawley

3D Freeshape Appliqué

This type of appliqué is designed to lay on the surface of a piece of work, hence the title of 3 Dimensional. Flowers and leaves look particularly good made in this method.

Method

◎ Use a design that doesn't have too many corners or points.

◎ Draw your motif on the top layer of fabric this line will be covered by stitching.

◎ Layer two fabrics together with wadding in between (batting) and pin avoiding the drawn lines

◎ Using a sewing machine with a walking foot, if you have one, (sometimes called an even feed foot), and selecting a medium size straight stitch, stitch around the motif on the drawn line, if you are competent at free machine embroidery or quilting then use that technique for stitching around the motif.

◎ Change your machine foot to an open toed appliqué foot if you have one - some models have a see through foot- and use a close zig-zag stitch or satin stitch to cover the straight stitched line.

◎ Cut out the shape close to the zig-zag stitching, don't worry if you cut some of the stitches, these will be covered on the next round.

◎ Next keep the stitch length of your zig-zag the same but widen the stitch width slightly and sew round the motif again, this round of stitching should cover the edge of the appliqué.

◎ Trim with scissors any straying strands of threads.

◎ Apply motif to your chosen background using hand stitches.

Tips

• Use a low-loft or cotton wadding (batting).
• Use the same fabric for the back and front of the appliqué.
• Make sure you have enough thread to complete a project, this method uses a lot of thread.
• Free machine embroidery or quilting involves lowering the feed dogs on the sewing machine, setting the stitch length to 0 and using a free machine embroidery foot or darning foot, you move the fabric to create the stitch, it takes some practice!

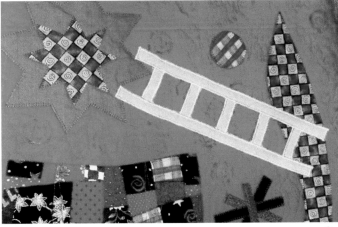

1   3D Freeshape Appliqué by Annette Morgan
2   3D Sample by Annette Morgan
3   'Snakes and Ladders' by Annette Morgan

Alicia Merrett

Alicia Merrett is originally from Buenos Aires, Argentina, and her passion for colour stems from growing up under intense blue skies, and in houses with gardens full of multicoloured flowers and birds. She studied South American culture and history at school, and learned at an early and impressionable age about the pre-Columbian cultures: Incas, Mayas and Aztecs. More recently she visited Mexico, and was greatly inspired by the imagery of those cultures, and also by the jungles and rain forests.

Alicia started to sew as a child but only returned to stitching once she had moved to Britain over 30 years ago. She has been a photographer and a professional toymaker and has written books on making cloth dolls and teddy bears.

Alicia started quilting in the mid 90's, the catalyst being an exhibition of contemporary American quilts at the Crafts Council in 1993. She then went on workshops in USA held by American tutors: Nancy Crow, Michael James, Caryl Bryer Fallert and Sue Benner. Last year she attended "The Quilt Design Symposium" in Columbus, Ohio, which offers four different courses over two weeks in June every year. Participants on the courses were selling fabrics and books in a mini-bazaar, where Alicia bought fabrics from Heide Stoll-Weber.

Although Alicia dyes some of her fabrics she prefers to use the multi-coloured cotton sateen produced by Heide, a German quilter and master dyer.

1 Alicia Merrett
2 'Traces of Ancient Kings' Detail by Alicia Merrett
3 'Elements of Magic' Detail 1 by Alicia Merrett
4 'Elements of Magic' by Alicia Merrett

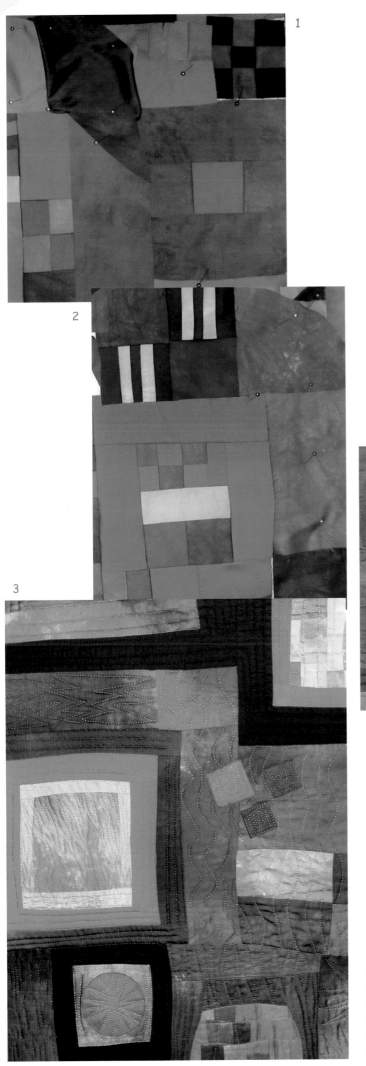

1 'Kaleidoscope' Work in Progress 1 by Alicia Merrett
2 'Kaleidoscope' Work in Progress 2 by Alicia Merrett
3 'Blue Planet Red Earth' Detail by Alicia Merrett
4 'Blue Planet Red Earth' by Alicia Merrett
5 'Blue Planet Red Earth' Detail by Alicia Merrett
6 'Explorations' by Alicia Merrett

Alicia makes mostly pieced quilts in an original, contemporary way, cutting the fabric free-hand with a rotary cutter without using a ruler. She sometimes adds shapes on the top layer of certain sections of a quilt, circles and squares are favourite embellishments. These are held in place by lines of quilting or by lines of straight machine stitching, using rayon thread which gives it a silvery shine. The shapes are often stitched through three layers, including wadding, which gives a raised 3D effect and from a distance the pieces appear to float. In "Traces of Ancient Kings", inspired by her trip to Mexico, Alicia applied shapes that had been fused with bonding fabric to a 'wholecloth' background.

In "Elements of Magic", based on concepts of beliefs in history and culture, Alicia used fused shapes and appliquéd them to small sections of fabric and wadding, joining them together to make a larger quilt. "Rain Gods and Plumed Serpents" uses 2 and 3 layers of fabric in a reverse appliqué technique, giving an almost 3D effect.

Alicia has recently started to use a technique called 'fused collage', which was pioneered in USA by Melody Johnson and Sue Benner. This method was used in "Windows on the World", where square shapes are appliquéd in an overlapping manner, fused by ironing and then quilted.

Technically, once the webbing has been ironed onto the back of the fabric, the paper backing is peeled off and the fabrics are ready for use. Shapes can now be cut as required, placed where wanted, and fused down with an iron. The completed work should always be stitched down or quilted to finish off.

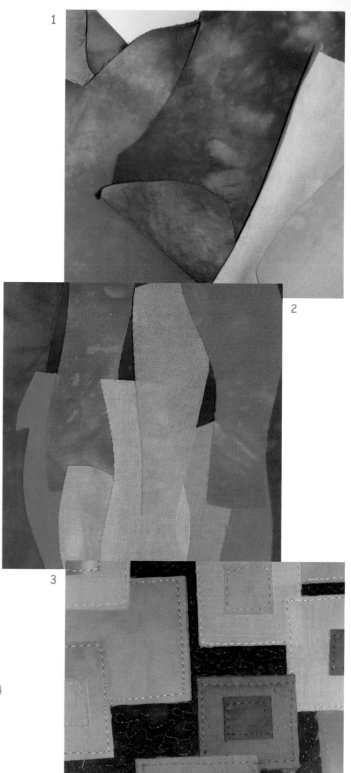

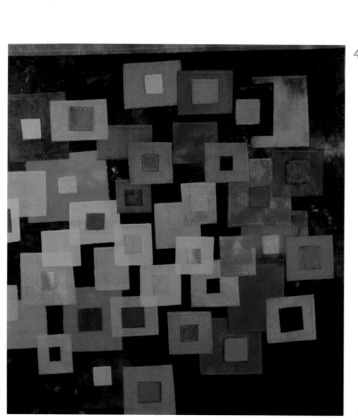

1   Fused Fabric Sample ready for use by Alicia Merrett
2   Fused Collage Sample by Alicia Merrett
3   'Windows of the World' Detail by Alicia Merrett
4   'Windows of the World' by Alicia Merrett

22

Sylvia Grant

Sylvia Grant has used the Kennet and Avon canal as the inspiration for her recent work. She lives near a very busy road and spends time under a bridge on the canal where it is quiet and there she is inspired by shapes of old bricks and water reflections.

In the textile piece 'Building Bridges 1', she has used a painted canvas background with minimal lines of stitching, then applied pieces of felt onto the surface. This is ready-made felt from a carpet factory, which has been dyed, boiled and distressed before application.

'Building Bridges 2' has a mesh background which was painted and covered to convey the man made structure of the canal bridge. On top of this are more pieces of ready-made felt applied at random.

Sylvia is interested in the tactile qualities in textiles and these pieces reflect that. They are an unusual use of appliqué but may inspire you to try some novel fabrics, plastics, mesh or found objects.

Val Holmes

Val Holmes, well known for her machine embroidery books, published by Batsford, uses a really simple form of appliqué in a very effective way. She cuts up squares of various fabrics, glitzy, sheers, plain fabrics, all in co-ordinating colours to fit with the theme of the work. These are laid down, slightly overlapping each other onto 'Solu Sheet'®, a dissolvable fabric or stuck to 'Aquabond'® sticky dissolvable fabric, which is secured in an embroidery ring. The surface is lightly machined down using a darning foot. Once the whole surface of the dissolvable sheet is covered in this way, Val machines into it with detailed machine stitch to integrate the surface more. The final stage is to dissolve the background fabric, leaving just the appliquéd fabrics and stitches to create the new fabric.

Val's latest book "The Encyclopedia of Machine Embroidery" was published by Batsford in late 2003.

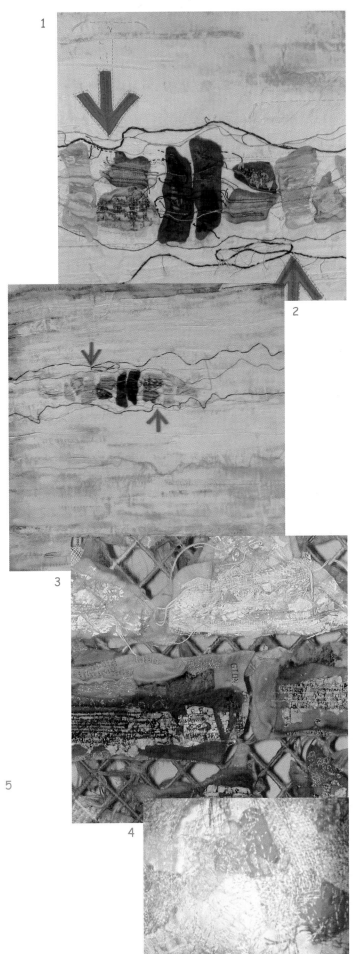

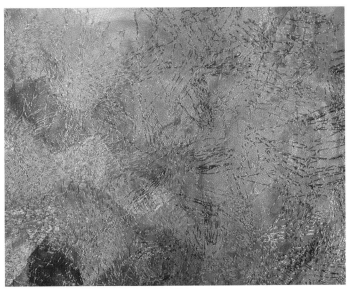

1 'Building Bridges' Detail by Sylvia Grant
2 'Building Bridges' by Sylvia Grant
3 'Building Bridges 2' by Sylvia Grant
4 Unfinished Sample by Val Holmes
5 Unfinished Sample by Val Holmes

Linda Kemshall

Linda Kemshall has used appliqué in her work for many years. She loves colour and enjoys using it in her work. She paints or dyes most of her fabrics, using hot water dyes and 'Procion' cold water dyes, colouring threads for quilting and stitching at the same time.

Linda uses bonding fabric for fused appliqué. Machine quilting is worked using decorative rayon threads. Hand quilting uses pure silk, cotton or linen hand dyed threads.

'Make your mark' - this quilt is pieced, with hand printing using a small cut sponge as a print block and acrylic paints. Foundation pieced shapes with bonded appliqué are added on top. This piece takes inspiration from a floral motif in a Paul Klee painting.

'Red Leaves' the background fabric of this quilt is shibori dyed with indigo. Leaves have been printed with disperse transfer dyes. The applied leaves are bonded then stitched. This piece was made to commemorate 200 years of the Royal Horticultural Society.

A Neil Young lyric provided the title for 'Hello, Ruby in the dust'. Simple piecing in a limited colour palette has been used to create the background fabric. Circles, which appear to float and squares have been applied to the surface and the quilt finally embellished with hand and machine stitching and enamelled metallic shapes.

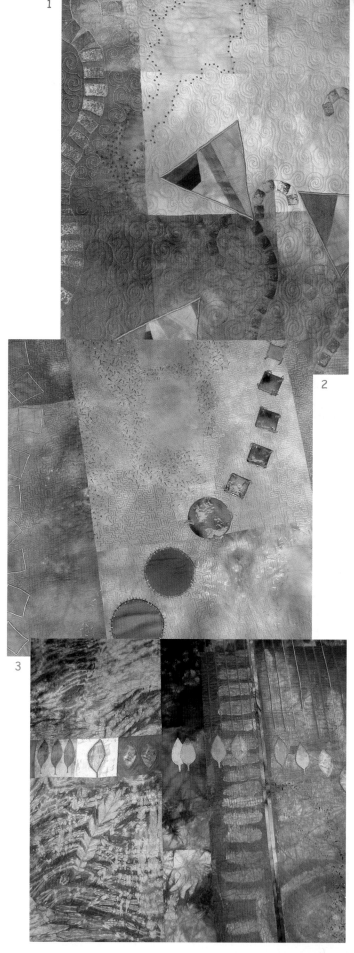

1   'Making Your Mark' by Linda Kemshall
2   'Hello Ruby in the Dust' Detail by Linda Kemshall
3   'Red Leaves' by Linda Kemshall
4   'Red Leaves' Detail by Linda Kemshall

Janice Myers

Janice Myers uses appliqué in a very unusual way. She applies one layer of plastic to another, using nylon fishing line to stitch in place. Janice buys large rolls of industrial polythene, she then cuts it into various shapes with a craft knife and often dyes the pieces with disperse or transfer dyes. Sometimes holes are punched in the pieces to give further pattern, these are then applied to the background plastic with stitch. The stitching is done with a darning needle using pliers to pull through the plastic. Janice says that she likes using unexpected materials with traditional techniques.

1 'Clear Cut' by Janice Myers
2 'x 2^2' by Janice Myers

Teresa Searle

Teresa Searle uses a lovely form of appliqué. She produces metres of pure woollen fabric on a knitting machine in various colours. Teresa particularly favours hot pinks, oranges and reds complementing the blues, purples and greens used. These are hot washed in a machine, felting the fabric by shrinking. These are then cutable without fraying, the shapes of bright flowers, birds and leaves are then applied to the knitted background fabric with zig-zag. Satin stitch, straight stitch and free machine embroidery are used to embellish the work.

Teresa's work has been seen at the Chelsea Craft Fair, the Knit & Stitch show in 2003 and has been featured in 'Country Living' and 'Crafts' magazines and is exhibited in various craft outlets.

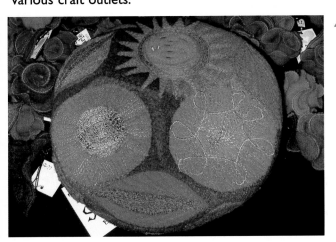

3 Hat by Teresa Searle
4 Knitted Jacket by Teresa Searle

Jan Mortimer

Jan Mortimer got her inspiration from the willows along the hedgerows and river banks around the area of Kingcombe in Dorset, where the textile group she belongs to meet to work. She worked from photographs, drawings, collages and paper studies. Her piece "Tangled Roots" uses applique by making small sections of ruched fabric, some-times wrapping and stuffing shapes then applying them to the surface. In another work "Tangled Roots and Branches" the appliquéd fabrics were enclosed inside a dyed area of woolen blanket.

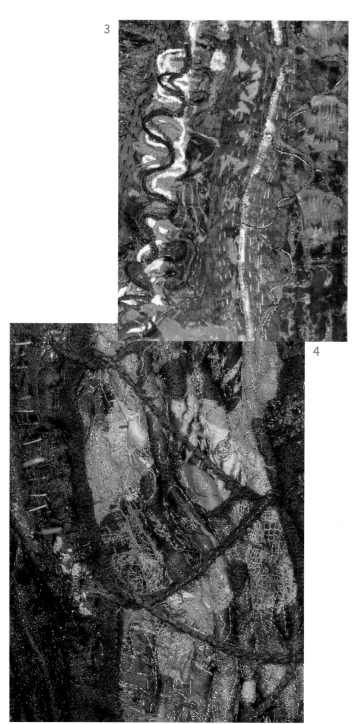

1 'Tangled Roots' by Jan Mortimer
2 'Tangled Roots and Branches' by Jan Mortimer
3 'Tangled Roots' Detail by Jan Mortimer
4 'Tangled Roots' Detail by Jan Mortimer

Penny Maishman

Penny Maishman got her inspiration from a photograph of rotting apples on her compost heap. This fitted with her theme of 'No beauty without decay'. The photograph was photocopied, enlarged, drawn into and re-photocopied. This was then cut up and used as a background which was covered with layers of fabric. The work "Rotting Apples" was made up of small pieces of hand-dyed cotton scrim, layers of lace, net and sheer fabrics. These were held down with machine stitch and then the whole surface was machine embroidered, indicating shadows and detail.

1 'Rotten Apples' Detail by Penny Maishman
2 'Rotten Apples 'Detail by Penny Maishman
3 'Rotten Apples' by Penny Maishman

27

Madeleine Millington

Madeleine Millington uses hand stitched blanket fabric for her quirky appliqué pieces. They all have a wonderful naive charm. Madeleine dyes recycled blanket fabric, which creates a rich spectrum of colour and texture. She cuts out shapes using pinking shears and then hand stitches using cotton perle or wool thread to the background blanket fabric. The pieces are worked in contemporary colours, embellished with ribbons, buttons and children's bead necklaces, tassles and torn fabric. Inspiration comes from an angel on a 12th century grave stone in the west country and other pieces depict faces, birds, fish or hearts. Having used hand stitch for a few years, Madeleine is now experimenting with machine stitching in her appliqué work.

1

2

3

4

5

1   'Little Angel' Blanket Fabric Appliqué by Madeleine Millington
2   'Orange Star' Blanket Fabric Appliqué by Madeleine Millington
3   'Celestial Soul' Blanket Fabric Appliqué by Madeleine Millington
4   Bag Detail Blanket Fabric Appliqué by Madeleine Millington
5   'Patchwork' Blanket Fabric Appliqué by Madeleine Millington

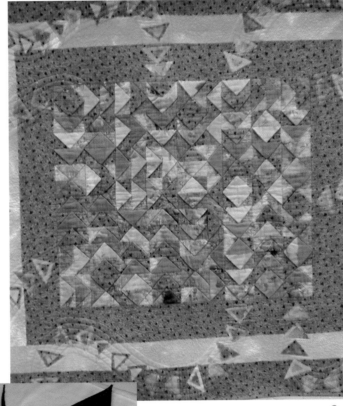

1

3

2

4

5

1 'Bowl' by Chris O'Dowd
2 'Setting the Goose Free' by Annette Morgan
3 'Container' by Allison Smith
4 'Grecian Lillies' by Annette Morgan
5 'Winter Journey' Detail by Annette Morgan

Resources

Book List

"The Art and Craft of Appliqué" - Juliet Bowden,
Mitchell Beazley ISBN 0 85533 921 7
"Appliqué" - Pauline Brown,
Merehurst Press, Embroidery Skills Series
ISBN 1 85391 058 9
"Appliqué" - Dorothy Tucker,
Batsford ISBN 0 7134 5349 4
The above are all out of print but may be found in
second hand bookshops.

"Contemporary Quilts" - Sandra Meech.
Batsford, October 2003 ISBN 0 7134 8856 5
"Patchwork, Quilting and Appliqué" - Linda Seward,
Mitchell Beazley ISBN 0-85533-663-3

Suppliers

'Bonda Webb' - Gillsew, Boundary House, Moor
Common, Lane End, Bucks. HP1 3HR Tel: 01494 881886,
email: gillsew@ukonline.co.uk

Freezer Paper, Invisible sewing thread, Bias tape making
tool, "Clover" mini iron etc.-Inca Studio, 10 Duke Street,
Princes Risborough, Bucks.
HP27 0AT Tel: 01844 343343, www.incastudio.com

'Super Mend' bonding powder - Rainbow Silks, 6
Wheelers Yard, High Street, Great Missenden, Bucks.
HP16 0AL
Tel: 01494 862111, www.rainbowsilks.co.uk

Fabrics - White & dyed; patterned, plains, all sorts -
Doughty's, 3 Capucin Yard, off Church Street, Hereford,
HR1 2LR Tel: 01432 265561 www.fabricsbydoughty.co.uk

White; calico, cotton in various weights, ready to dye -
Whaleys (Bradford) Ltd. Harris Court, Great Horton,
Bradford, W. Yorks. BD7 4EQ
Tel: 01274 576718 www.whaleys-bradford.ltd.uk

Dyes - Omega Dyes, Myrtle Cottage, Powerstock,
Bridport, DT6 3TD Tel: 01308 485242
www.omegadyes.co.uk

Art Van Go, The Studios, 1 Stevenage Road,
Knebworth, Herts. SG3 6AN
Tel:01438 814946 www.artvango.co.uk

Web sites worth visiting
www.annettemorgan.co.uk
www.baileycurtis.com
www.lindakemshall.com
www.linda-straw-quilts.co.uk

1

2

1 'Medieval Tiles' by Annette Morgan
2 'Medieval Tiles' Detail by Annette Morgan

Bailey Curtis

Bailey has been working in textiles for over 30 years. She started as a weaver, spinner and dyer with a Diploma in those from Bradford College of Art & Technology. She then discovered feltmaking 19 years ago, followed by embroidery and obtained City & Guilds, Embroidery part 1, City & Guilds, Creative Textiles part 2, and a Diploma from East Berkshire College in Stitched Textiles.

During the last 12 years Bailey has been teaching A Level, Art & Design-Textiles and running a mail order business selling a range of dyes. She wrote and published her first book "Dyeing To Colour" in 2001, the second, "Inspiration To Stitch" in 2003.

Bailey has a life-long interest in textiles, which started in childhood. Her work now is nearly all felt with cotton appliqué which is all dyed, sometimes before the work is put together, other times the whole piece is put together then dip-dyed. She calls herself 'an accidental quilter', mainly because her work is layered wool with a cotton backing. Inspired by the landscape around her, Bailey's work is mainly shown in stitched textile exhibitions in the UK and in USA, also a few quilt shows.

Annette Morgan

Annette Morgan is a national and international quiltmaker who has been invited to exhibit her work in America, Japan and Europe. She teaches extensively in the UK, particularly City & Guilds courses to Diploma level.

Annette was President of the Quilters Guild of The British Isles from 2001 to 2003 and it was her suggestion to found the Contemporary Quilt Group. She is co-founder and member of Anglia Textile Works.

Annette lives in Suffolk, having spent most of her life in East Anglia and is inspired by the surrounding landscape.

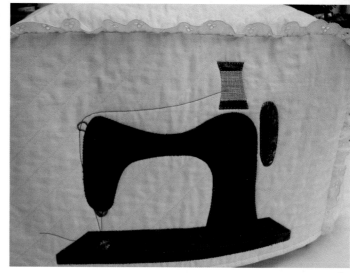

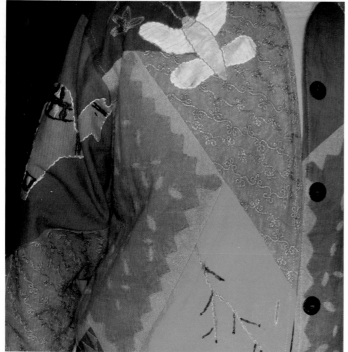

1

4

2

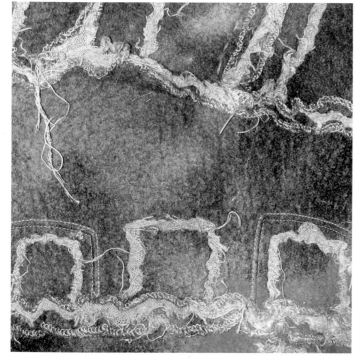

6

3

1 'Indian Jacket'
2 'Powis Castle Gardens' Detail by Bailey Curtis
3 'Hat' by Allison Smith
4 Sewing Machine Cover by Cathy Cruthirds
5 'A Taste of Summer" by Annette Morgan
6 'Bodnant Gardens' Detail by Bailey Curtis